advanced plumbing techniques

A Comprehensive Guide to Tackling Complex Projects for the DIY Enthusiast

harper wells

life level up books, llc.

contents

Introduction	v
1. Advanced Techniques for Pipe Installation and Replacement	1
2. Advanced Fixture Installations	13
3. Advanced Drainage and Venting Techniques	27
4. Complex Water Supply System Repairs and Installations	41
5. Advanced Troubleshooting and Problem-Solving	57
6. Plumbing for Home Additions and Renovations	75
Conclusion	89

Advanced Plumbing Techniques: A Comprehensive Guide to Tackling Complex Projects for the DIY Enthusiast

Copyright © 2023 by Harper Wells

Copyright © 2023 by Life Level Up Books, LLC

All rights reserved.

Disclaimer Notice:

Please note the information contained within this document is for educational and entertainment purposes only. All effort has been executed to present accurate, up to date, reliable, complete information. No warranties of any kind are declared or implied. Readers acknowledge that the author is not engaged in the rendering of legal, financial, medical or professional advice. The content within this book has been derived from various sources. Please consult a licensed professional before attempting any techniques outlined in this book.

By reading this document, the reader agrees that under no circumstances is the author responsible for any losses, direct or indirect, that are incurred as a result of the use of the information contained within this document, including, but not limited to, errors, omissions, or inaccuracies.

This book is written for entertainment purposes only. The statements made in this book do not necessarily reflect the present market at the time of reading or current views of the author. Furthermore, the author accepts no responsibility for actions taken by the reader as a result of information presented in this book.

No part of this book may be reproduced in any form or by any electronic or mechanical means, including information storage and retrieval systems, without written permission from the author, except for the use of brief quotations in a book review.

introduction

Introduction

The Importance of Advanced Plumbing Skills for Professionals and Homeowners

Advanced plumbing skills are essential for professionals and homeowners alike, as they provide the ability to tackle complex projects, ensure proper system functioning, and maintain a safe and efficient plumbing system. In this section, we will discuss the importance of advanced plumbing skills for both professionals and homeowners.

Increased Competence and Confidence: Developing advanced plumbing skills allows professionals and homeowners to tackle a wider range of projects with greater competence and confidence. This leads to higher quality work and reduces the likelihood of mistakes and costly repairs.

Greater Efficiency and Effectiveness: Advanced skills enable plumbers to work more efficiently and effectively, which can result in faster project completion times, fewer callbacks, and higher customer satisfaction.

Enhanced Problem-Solving Abilities: With a strong foundation in advanced plumbing techniques, professionals and homeowners can better diagnose and troubleshoot complex issues, finding innovative solutions that might not be apparent to those with only basic skills.

Adherence to Building Codes and Regulations: Advanced plumbing skills ensure that professionals and homeowners are knowledgeable about current building codes and regulations. This is critical for maintaining a safe and compliant plumbing system and avoiding penalties or fines.

Improved Safety and Health: Properly functioning plumbing systems are essential for maintaining a safe and healthy living environment. Advanced plumbing skills can help prevent issues

Introduction

such as leaks, water damage, mold growth, and sewer gas infiltration, which can pose health risks and compromise the structural integrity of a building.

Cost Savings: By possessing advanced plumbing skills, professionals and homeowners can save money on repairs and maintenance by addressing issues early or completing projects themselves rather than hiring outside help.

Increased Property Value: A well-maintained and properly functioning plumbing system can significantly increase the value of a property. Advanced plumbing skills can help ensure that systems are up-to-date, efficient, and reliable, making a property more attractive to potential buyers.

Environmental Benefits: Advanced plumbing skills can contribute to more environmentally friendly plumbing systems, such as the efficient use of water resources and the proper disposal of waste materials. This can help reduce a property's environmental footprint and contribute to a more sustainable future.

Professional Growth and Career Opportunities: For professionals, mastering advanced plumbing skills can lead to new career opportunities, such as promotions, increased responsibilities, or starting their own business. Additionally, it can enhance their reputation in the industry and make them more appealing to potential clients.

Empowerment and Self-Sufficiency: For homeowners, having advanced plumbing skills can provide a sense of empowerment and self-sufficiency, allowing them to address issues and complete projects without relying on outside help.

The importance of advanced plumbing skills cannot be overstated. By investing in the development of these skills, both

Introduction

professionals and homeowners can reap numerous benefits, including increased competence, cost savings, and improved safety and health.

Introduction

Safety Precautions and Best Practices for Plumbing Professionals and Homeowners

Ensuring safety while working on plumbing projects is crucial to prevent accidents, injuries, and damage to property. Here, we discuss safety precautions and best practices that plumbing professionals and homeowners should follow:

Personal Protective Equipment (PPE): Wear appropriate PPE, including safety glasses, gloves, and sturdy footwear, to protect yourself from potential hazards like sharp tools, chemicals, and hot or cold surfaces.

Proper Tool Use and Maintenance: Always use the right tool for the task at hand and keep them in good working condition. Misusing tools or using damaged ones can lead to accidents and injuries.

Turning Off Water Supply: Before starting any plumbing work, turn off the water supply to the area you'll be working on. This helps prevent water damage, flooding, and potential accidents caused by high water pressure.

Ventilation: Ensure adequate ventilation when working in confined spaces or with chemicals, like solvents or adhesives. Proper ventilation helps prevent the buildup of hazardous fumes, which can cause respiratory issues or fire hazards.

Electrical Safety: Always be cautious when working near electrical wiring or components. Turn off the power supply to the area you're working on and use a non-contact voltage tester to confirm it's safe to proceed. Be mindful of the potential for water and electricity to come into contact, as this can result in electrocution.

Lifting and Carrying Techniques: Follow proper lifting and carrying techniques to avoid injuries, especially when handling

Introduction

heavy materials or equipment. Bend your knees, keep your back straight, and use your legs to lift, avoiding any twisting motions.

Ladder Safety: When using a ladder, ensure it's on a stable and level surface, and follow the manufacturer's guidelines for weight limits and proper use. Always maintain three points of contact (two hands and one foot, or two feet and one hand) while climbing or descending.

Awareness of Gas Lines: Be cautious when working near gas lines. Accidentally puncturing or damaging a gas line can lead to gas leaks or explosions. Familiarize yourself with the location of gas lines in the area you're working on and take extra care when drilling or cutting.

Emergency Preparedness: Keep a well-stocked first aid kit and fire extinguisher on hand during plumbing projects. Know the location of emergency shut-off valves for water, gas, and electricity, and be prepared to use them in case of accidents or emergencies.

Training and Skill Development: Continuously invest in training and skill development to stay up-to-date with the latest safety standards, best practices, and techniques. This includes participating in workshops, courses, and industry events, as well as staying informed about changes in building codes and regulations.

By following these safety precautions and best practices, plumbing professionals and homeowners can minimize the risk of accidents, injuries, and damage to property, ensuring a safe and successful plumbing project.

Introduction

Tools and Materials Required for Complex Plumbing Projects

When undertaking complex plumbing projects, having the right tools and materials is crucial for successful completion. Here, we provide a list of essential tools and materials needed for most complex plumbing projects:

Pipe Cutters: Different types of pipe cutters, such as tubing cutters, hacksaws, and reciprocating saws, are essential for cutting various pipe materials, including copper, PVC, CPVC, and ABS.

Pipe Wrenches: Adjustable pipe wrenches are necessary for tightening and loosening threaded pipes, fittings, and valves.

Pipe Benders: Pipe benders help create smooth, consistent bends in copper and other soft metal pipes without causing kinks or damage.

Press Fitting Tools: Press fitting tools are used for creating leak-proof connections in PEX and copper pipes without the need for soldering or gluing.

Pipe Threading and Tapping Tools: These tools are used for cutting threads on pipes and creating threaded holes for valves, fittings, and fixtures.

Pipe Vises and Stands: Pipe vises and stands are essential for securely holding pipes in place while cutting, threading, or soldering.

Plungers and Augers: These tools help clear clogs and blockages in drains, toilets, and sewer lines.

Inspection Cameras and Locators: Inspection cameras and pipe locators assist in identifying and locating leaks, blockages, and other issues within pipes that are not easily accessible.

Introduction

Soldering and Brazing Equipment: For projects involving copper pipes, you'll need a propane or acetylene torch, solder, flux, and brazing rods to create watertight connections.

PPE (Personal Protective Equipment): Safety glasses, gloves, and sturdy footwear are essential for protecting yourself from potential hazards while working on complex plumbing projects.

Pipe Supports and Hangers: These materials help secure and support pipes, ensuring proper alignment and preventing sagging or movement.

Pipe and Fitting Materials: Depending on the project, you may require various pipe materials (copper, PVC, CPVC, ABS, PEX) and corresponding fittings, valves, and connectors.

Sealants and Adhesives: Teflon tape, pipe dope, and pipe cement are necessary for creating watertight seals in threaded or glued pipe connections.

Pressure and Temperature Gauges: These gauges help monitor and diagnose issues related to water pressure and temperature in plumbing systems.

Pipe Insulation and Heat Tape: Insulation and heat tape help protect pipes from freezing, reduce condensation, and maintain consistent temperatures in hot water lines.

Measuring and Marking Tools: Tape measures, levels, and markers are essential for accurately measuring and marking pipes and fittings during installation.

Pipe Cleaning and Maintenance Supplies: Pipe brushes, descalers, and water jetting equipment help clean and maintain pipes to prevent blockages and ensure proper flow.

Water and Gas Shut-Off Tools: These tools, such as water meter keys and gas shut-off wrenches, are crucial for safely turning off water or gas supplies during plumbing projects.

By having the right tools and materials on hand, plumbing professionals and homeowners can effectively tackle complex plumbing projects while ensuring efficiency, safety, and quality workmanship. Ready to dive into the world of advanced plumbing? Let's get started...

Introduction

WANT FREE BOOKS?

FREEBOOKDAILY.COM

SOLARTURNSMEON.COM

SKY HIGH ENERGY BILL?

Stop Renting Your Energy, Own It Just Like You Own Your Home

- Solar for **$0 down**
- **Save up to $200/mo** on energy
- **Increase** your home value
- Get **clean renewable energy**
- Get a **30-year warranty**
- **Customized** proposal & best value

advanced techniques for pipe installation and replacement
. . .

Working with Different Pipe Materials: Unlock the Potential of Copper, PVC, CPVC, and ABS in Your Advanced Plumbing Projects

ARE you ready to take your plumbing skills to the next level? In this subchapter, we'll delve into the fascinating world of copper, PVC, CPVC, and ABS pipes, ensuring that you can confidently tackle any plumbing project that comes your way. Let's dive in and explore these versatile materials and their unique properties.

Copper: The Classic Choice

COPPER HAS BEEN a favorite among plumbers for decades, and for good reason! This reliable, durable material is not only easy to work with but also resistant to corrosion and leaks. As you begin your project, you'll find that copper pipes come in various thicknesses (Type M, L, and K), providing you with the flexibility to choose the right one for your needs. When working with copper, you'll become proficient in soldering and cutting techniques, allowing you to create secure, leak-free connections. Embrace the artistry and craftsmanship behind copper plumbing and watch your projects stand the test of time!

PVC: The Lightweight Champion

PVC (POLYVINYL CHLORIDE) pipes offer a lightweight, affordable, and low-maintenance alternative to copper. Their smooth interior surface promotes excellent water flow, reducing the chances of clogs and blockages. Perfect for drainage and venting applications, PVC pipes can be easily cut and joined using solvent cement, simplifying the installation process. Keep in mind that PVC is sensitive to UV rays and should not be used for outdoor projects exposed to sunlight. However, for indoor applications, PVC is an excellent choice that will have you marveling at your handiwork for years to come.

CPVC: The Heat-Resistant Innovator

CPVC (CHLORINATED Polyvinyl Chloride) pipes are a game-changing addition to your plumbing repertoire. With higher temperature resistance than PVC, CPVC is perfect for hot water supply lines. Its durability and low cost make it an attractive option for both residential and commercial applications. Like PVC, CPVC pipes can be easily cut and joined using solvent cement, streamlining your project and reducing the likelihood of errors. By choosing CPVC, you'll showcase your ability to stay ahead of the curve and adapt to new plumbing technologies.

ABS: The Tough and Resilient Performer

ABS (ACRYLONITRILE BUTADIENE STYRENE) pipes are the unsung heroes of the plumbing world, boasting exceptional strength and impact resistance. Ideal for underground drainage systems, ABS pipes can withstand harsh conditions without compromising performance. Their lightweight nature and simple installation process—using solvent cement to create strong bonds—make them an appealing choice for DIY enthusiasts. By incorporating ABS pipes into your projects, you'll demonstrate your commitment to quality and resilience, ensuring that your plumbing system remains in peak condition.

UNDERSTANDING the nuances of different pipe materials—copper, PVC, CPVC, and ABS—will empower you to make informed decisions for your advanced plumbing projects. With this knowledge at your fingertips, you'll be able to tackle any plumbing challenge with confidence and enthusiasm. Embrace the exciting world of pipe materials and watch as your projects transform from simple fixes to awe-inspiring masterpieces. Happy plumbing!

Pipe Soldering and Brazing Techniques: Mastering the Art of Secure and Durable Connections

A SOLID AND reliable plumbing system hinges on strong connections, which is why mastering the techniques of pipe soldering and brazing is essential for any DIY enthusiast. Let's explore these methods and unlock your potential to create leak-free, lasting pipe connections.

Pipe Soldering: The Reliable Bond

SOLDERING IS a popular technique for joining copper pipes, valued for its strong, leak-proof connections. To become proficient in pipe soldering, follow these steps:

PREPARING THE PIPES: Before soldering, clean the pipe ends and fitting interiors with a wire brush or sandpaper. This ensures a clean surface for the solder to bond properly.

APPLYING FLUX: Apply a thin layer of flux to the cleaned areas. Flux is a chemical agent that facilitates solder flow and prevents oxidation during the soldering process.

FITTING THE PIPES: Insert the pipe into the fitting, ensuring a snug connection. Wipe off any excess flux with a damp cloth to prevent corrosion.

HEATING THE CONNECTION: Using a propane torch, evenly heat the connection area until the flux begins to sizzle. The key is to heat the fitting, not the pipe, allowing the heat to transfer and distribute evenly.

APPLYING SOLDER: Touch the solder to the joint, letting it flow and fill the gap by capillary action. Remove the heat and allow the solder to cool and solidify, creating a watertight seal.

COOLING AND CLEANING: Let the joint cool naturally—avoid using water or other cooling agents. Once cooled, clean any remaining flux residue with a damp cloth to prevent future corrosion.

Pipe Brazing: The High-Strength Alternative

BRAZING, a technique similar to soldering, utilizes a filler metal with a higher melting point, creating an even stronger bond. This method is ideal for heavy-duty plumbing applications. To excel in pipe brazing, follow these steps:

PREPARING THE PIPES: Clean the pipe ends and fitting interiors using a wire brush or sandpaper to create a smooth, debris-free surface.

APPLYING FLUX: Coat the cleaned areas with brazing flux to prevent oxidation and promote smooth filler metal flow.

FITTING THE PIPES: Join the pipe and fitting, ensuring a tight connection. Remove any excess flux to prevent joint contamination.

. . .

HEATING THE CONNECTION: Using an oxy-acetylene torch, evenly heat the connection area. Brazing requires higher temperatures than soldering, so focus the flame on the fitting and the pipe in a sweeping motion to distribute heat evenly.

APPLYING BRAZING ROD: Touch the brazing rod to the heated joint, allowing the filler metal to melt and flow into the gap by capillary action. Remove the heat and let the brazed joint cool and solidify.

COOLING AND CLEANING: Allow the joint to cool naturally. Once cooled, clean any remaining flux residue with a damp cloth or wire brush to avoid corrosion.

BY MASTERING both soldering and brazing techniques, you'll be well-equipped to handle various pipe-joining situations with confidence. These skills will elevate your plumbing projects, ensuring secure and long-lasting connections that stand the test of time.

Pipe Threading and Joining Methods: Unleash the Power of Strong and Dependable Connections

CREATING secure and lasting connections is paramount in any plumbing project. In this section, we'll explore the exciting world of pipe threading and various joining methods, enabling you to tackle diverse plumbing challenges with ease.

Pipe Threading: Precision Meets Functionality

PIPE THREADING IS a technique used for joining metal pipes, such as galvanized steel or black iron. Threading creates a strong, reliable connection that can be disassembled if necessary. Let's delve into the process of threading pipes:

CUTTING THREADS: Using a pipe threader, either manual or electric, cut the threads onto the end of the pipe. Ensure that the die is sharp and well-maintained to create clean, precise threads.

PREPARING THE THREADS: Clean the newly-cut threads with a wire brush, removing any burrs or debris. Apply pipe joint compound or thread seal tape to the threads, which helps to lubricate and seal the connection.

JOINING THE PIPES: Carefully screw the threaded pipe end into the corresponding fitting, ensuring that the threads engage properly. Tighten the connection with a pipe wrench until secure but avoid over-tightening, which can cause damage or leaks.

Popular Joining Methods: A World of Possibilities

IN ADDITION TO THREADING, there are several other methods for joining pipes. These techniques provide versatility and adaptability in your plumbing projects.

COMPRESSION FITTINGS: These fittings use a compression nut and a ring, or ferrule, to create a watertight seal. Compression fittings are great for joining copper, PEX, or CPVC pipes without soldering or gluing. Tighten the nut until secure, and you'll have a strong, leak-free connection.

PUSH-FIT FITTINGS: Push-fit fittings are designed for quick and easy connections without the need for tools or additional materials. Ideal for copper, PEX, and CPVC pipes, simply insert the pipe into the fitting until it clicks into place, ensuring a watertight seal.

FLARED FITTINGS: Flared fittings are primarily used with soft copper pipes, providing a strong, leak-resistant connection. To use flared fittings, first flare the pipe end using a flaring tool. Then, insert the flared pipe end into the fitting and tighten the connection with a flare nut.

PEX CRIMP AND EXPANSION FITTINGS: PEX pipes utilize specialized crimp or expansion fittings, which are designed for secure and leak-free connections. Crimp fittings require a crimping tool to compress a metal ring around the pipe and fitting, while expansion fittings use an expansion tool to enlarge the PEX pipe before inserting a fitting with a sealing ring.

. . .

By familiarizing yourself with pipe threading and various joining methods, you'll be well-prepared to handle any plumbing project that comes your way. These techniques will enable you to create strong, reliable connections that enhance the performance and longevity of your plumbing system.

**Need Plumbing Help?
Grab The Companion Books
By Harper Wells**

advanced fixture installations
· · ·

Installing Luxury Shower Systems: Transform Your Bathroom into a Spa-like Sanctuary

A LUXURY SHOWER system can elevate your bathroom experience, providing relaxation, rejuvenation, and a touch of sophistication. In this section, we'll guide you through the process of installing a luxury shower system, turning your bathroom into a personal oasis.

Planning and Design

BEFORE DIVING INTO THE INSTALLATION, consider the following aspects to ensure a successful project:

SHOWER SYSTEM TYPE: Choose the ideal shower system for your needs and preferences. Options include rain showers, body sprays, handheld showerheads, and even digital controls for a truly customized experience.

SPACE AND LAYOUT: Measure your shower area and determine the optimal placement for each component, considering factors such as water pressure, pipe access, and user preferences.

PLUMBING AND ELECTRICAL REQUIREMENTS: Luxury shower systems may require additional plumbing or electrical modifications, such as dedicated water lines, valves, or electrical outlets. Consult local building codes and consider hiring a professional if needed.

Preparing for Installation

Advanced Plumbing Techniques

ONCE THE DESIGN IS FINALIZED, gather the necessary tools and materials, such as wrenches, drills, anchors, and Teflon tape. Turn off the water supply and electricity to the bathroom before starting any work.

Mounting the Shower Components

FOLLOW these steps to install the various components of your luxury shower system:

SHOWERHEAD AND ARM: Install the shower arm by threading it into the water supply pipe and securing it with Teflon tape. Attach the showerhead to the shower arm, ensuring a snug fit.

BODY SPRAYS: Mark the desired locations for the body sprays on the shower wall. Drill holes and install the mounting brackets or rough-in valves according to the manufacturer's instructions. Attach the body sprays to the brackets or valves, ensuring secure connections.

HANDHELD SHOWERHEAD: Install the mounting bracket for the handheld showerhead at a convenient height and location. Attach the shower hose to the water supply outlet and the handheld showerhead, securing the connections with Teflon tape.

CONTROLS AND VALVES: Install the thermostatic or pressure-balancing valve and diverter valve following the manufacturer's guidelines. Mount the control panel or knobs at a comfortable height and connect them to the valves.

Connecting the Plumbing

WITH ALL COMPONENTS MOUNTED, connect the water supply lines to the shower system, ensuring secure connections. Install any additional pipes or fittings necessary to accommodate the new shower components.

Testing and Fine-tuning

TURN on the water supply and electricity to the bathroom. Test the shower system for proper function, checking for leaks and adjusting the water pressure or temperature as needed.

Finishing Touches

APPLY caulk or silicone sealant around the shower components to prevent water infiltration. Reinstall any wall panels or tiles removed during the installation process.

CONGRATULATIONS! With your luxury shower system now installed, you've transformed your bathroom into a spa-like retreat. Enjoy the indulgent experience and take pride in your impressive DIY accomplishment!

Installing Whirlpool Tubs and Spa Baths: Immerse Yourself in Relaxation and Luxury

A WHIRLPOOL TUB or spa bath can enhance your bathing experience, providing soothing hydrotherapy and a touch of opulence. In this section, we'll guide you through the process of installing a whirlpool tub or spa bath, transforming your bathroom into a haven of relaxation.

Planning and Design

BEFORE BEGINNING THE INSTALLATION, consider the following aspects to ensure a successful project:

TUB TYPE AND SIZE: Choose the ideal whirlpool tub or spa bath that suits your needs and bathroom dimensions. Options include drop-in, alcove, corner, or freestanding tubs with various jet configurations and features.

SPACE AND LAYOUT: Measure your bathroom and determine the optimal placement for the tub, considering factors such as plumbing access, electrical requirements, and user preferences.

PLUMBING AND ELECTRICAL REQUIREMENTS: Whirlpool tubs and spa baths may require additional plumbing or electrical modifications, such as dedicated water lines, drains, or GFCI-protected outlets. Consult local building codes and consider hiring a professional if needed.

Preparing for Installation

ONCE THE DESIGN IS FINALIZED, gather the necessary tools and materials, such as wrenches, drills, anchors, and a carpenter's level. Turn off the water supply and electricity to the bathroom before starting any work.

Removing the Old Tub (if applicable)

IF YOU'RE REPLACING AN EXISTING tub, disconnect the plumbing fixtures and drain, then carefully remove the old tub from the bathroom. Clean and inspect the area, making any necessary repairs to the flooring, walls, or plumbing.

Assembling and Positioning the Tub

FOLLOW the manufacturer's instructions to assemble the whirlpool tub or spa bath, which may include attaching the legs, skirt, or pump. Position the tub in the desired location, ensuring that it is level and aligned with the plumbing connections.

Connecting the Plumbing

WITH THE TUB IN PLACE, connect the water supply lines and drain to the tub's fixtures, ensuring secure connections. Install any additional pipes or fittings necessary to accommodate the new whirlpool tub or spa bath.

Connecting the Electrical Components

WHIRLPOOL TUBS and spa baths typically require a dedicated GFCI-protected circuit for the pump and any additional features, such as heaters or lights. Consult the manufacturer's guidelines for the proper electrical setup and consider hiring a licensed electrician to ensure safe and code-compliant installation.

Testing and Fine-tuning

TURN on the water supply and electricity to the bathroom. Fill the tub and test the whirlpool or spa functions for proper operation, checking for leaks and adjusting the water pressure or temperature as needed.

Finishing Touches

APPLY caulk or silicone sealant around the tub to prevent water infiltration. Reinstall any wall panels, tiles, or trim removed during the installation process.

WITH YOUR WHIRLPOOL tub or spa bath now installed, you've created a sanctuary of relaxation and luxury in your own bathroom. Enjoy the soothing hydrotherapy experience and take pride in your impressive DIY achievement!

Integrating Smart Faucets and Fixtures: Embrace Convenience and Efficiency in Your Bathroom

SMART FAUCETS and fixtures bring modern technology to your bathroom, offering enhanced functionality, water conservation, and a touch of sophistication. In this section, we'll guide you through the process of integrating smart faucets and fixtures, transforming your bathroom into a cutting-edge, eco-friendly space.

Planning and Design

BEFORE BEGINNING THE INTEGRATION PROCESS, consider the following aspects to ensure a successful project:

FIXTURE TYPE AND FEATURES: Choose the ideal smart faucets and fixtures that meet your needs and preferences. Options include touchless faucets, digital shower controls, automatic soap dispensers, and intelligent toilets with various features like temperature control, water conservation, and voice activation.

SPACE AND LAYOUT: Measure your bathroom and determine the optimal placement for each smart fixture, considering factors such as plumbing access, electrical requirements, and user preferences.

PLUMBING AND ELECTRICAL REQUIREMENTS: Smart faucets and fixtures may require additional plumbing or electrical modifications, such as dedicated water lines, valves, or GFCI-protected outlets. Consult local building codes and consider hiring a professional if needed.

Preparing for Installation

ONCE THE DESIGN IS FINALIZED, gather the necessary tools and materials, such as wrenches, drills, anchors, and a carpenter's level. Turn off the water supply and electricity to the bathroom before starting any work.

Removing the Old Fixtures (if applicable)

IF YOU'RE REPLACING EXISTING fixtures, disconnect the plumbing and electrical connections, then carefully remove the old fixtures from the bathroom. Clean and inspect the area, making any necessary repairs to the walls, plumbing, or wiring.

Installing the Smart Faucets and Fixtures

FOLLOW the manufacturer's instructions to install each smart faucet or fixture, ensuring proper alignment with the plumbing connections and a secure fit.

SMART FAUCETS: Attach the faucet to the sink or countertop, and connect the water supply lines and any electrical wiring required. Install the control box, sensor, or battery pack according to the manufacturer's guidelines.

DIGITAL SHOWER CONTROLS: Mount the digital control panel at a convenient height and location, and connect it to the water supply lines, valves, and any electrical wiring required.

. . .

Automatic Soap Dispensers: Install the soap dispenser on the countertop or wall, and connect any required electrical wiring or batteries. Fill the dispenser with the appropriate soap or sanitizer.

Intelligent Toilets: Position the toilet in the desired location, ensuring that it is level and aligned with the plumbing connections. Attach the toilet to the floor flange, and connect the water supply line and any electrical wiring required.

Testing and Fine-tuning

Turn on the water supply and electricity to the bathroom. Test the smart faucets and fixtures for proper operation, checking for leaks, and adjusting settings as needed. Some fixtures may require syncing with a smartphone app or voice assistant for additional customization.

Finishing Touches

Apply caulk or silicone sealant around the fixtures to prevent water infiltration. Reinstall any wall panels, tiles, or trim removed during the installation process.

Congratulations! By integrating smart faucets and fixtures, you've created a modern, eco-friendly bathroom that combines convenience, efficiency, and style. Enjoy the advanced features and take pride in your impressive DIY accomplishment!

Installing Bidets and Advanced Toilet Systems: Enhance Your Bathroom Experience with Ultimate Comfort and Hygiene

BIDETS and advanced toilet systems offer superior hygiene, comfort, and convenience, transforming your bathroom experience. In this section, we'll guide you through the process of installing bidets and advanced toilet systems, elevating your bathroom to a new level of luxury and cleanliness.

Planning and Design

BEFORE BEGINNING THE INSTALLATION, consider the following aspects to ensure a successful project:

BIDET TYPE AND FEATURES: Choose the ideal bidet or advanced toilet system that suits your needs and preferences. Options include standalone bidets, bidet seats, or integrated bidet-toilet combinations with various features such as heated seats, air dryers, and customizable spray settings.

SPACE AND LAYOUT: Measure your bathroom and determine the optimal placement for the bidet or advanced toilet system, considering factors such as plumbing access, electrical requirements, and user preferences.

PLUMBING AND ELECTRICAL REQUIREMENTS: Bidets and advanced toilet systems may require additional plumbing or electrical modifications, such as dedicated water lines, drains, or GFCI-protected outlets. Consult local building codes and consider hiring a professional if needed.

Preparing for Installation

ONCE THE DESIGN IS FINALIZED, gather the necessary tools and materials, such as wrenches, drills, anchors, and a carpenter's level. Turn off the water supply and electricity to the bathroom before starting any work.

Removing the Old Toilet (if applicable)

IF YOU'RE REPLACING AN EXISTING toilet, disconnect the water supply line and drain, then carefully remove the old toilet from the bathroom. Clean and inspect the area, making any necessary repairs to the flooring, walls, or plumbing.

Installing the Bidet or Advanced Toilet System

FOLLOW the manufacturer's instructions to install the bidet or advanced toilet system, ensuring proper alignment with the plumbing connections and a secure fit.

STANDALONE BIDETS: Position the bidet in the desired location, ensuring that it is level and aligned with the plumbing connections. Attach the bidet to the floor flange, and connect the water supply line and drain.

BIDET SEATS: Remove the existing toilet seat, and attach the bidet seat to the toilet bowl according to the manufacturer's guidelines. Connect the water supply line and any electrical wiring required.

. . .

INTEGRATED BIDET-TOILET COMBINATIONS: Position the bidet-toilet combination in the desired location, ensuring that it is level and aligned with the plumbing connections. Attach the unit to the floor flange, and connect the water supply line, drain, and any electrical wiring required.

Testing and Fine-tuning

TURN on the water supply and electricity to the bathroom. Test the bidet or advanced toilet system for proper operation, checking for leaks and adjusting settings as needed. Some systems may require syncing with a smartphone app or remote control for additional customization.

Finishing Touches

APPLY caulk or silicone sealant around the bidet or advanced toilet system to prevent water infiltration. Reinstall any wall panels, tiles, or trim removed during the installation process.

WITH YOUR BIDET or advanced toilet system now installed, you've created a luxurious and hygienic bathroom environment. Enjoy the enhanced comfort and cleanliness, and take pride in your impressive DIY accomplishment!

advanced drainage and venting techniques
. . .

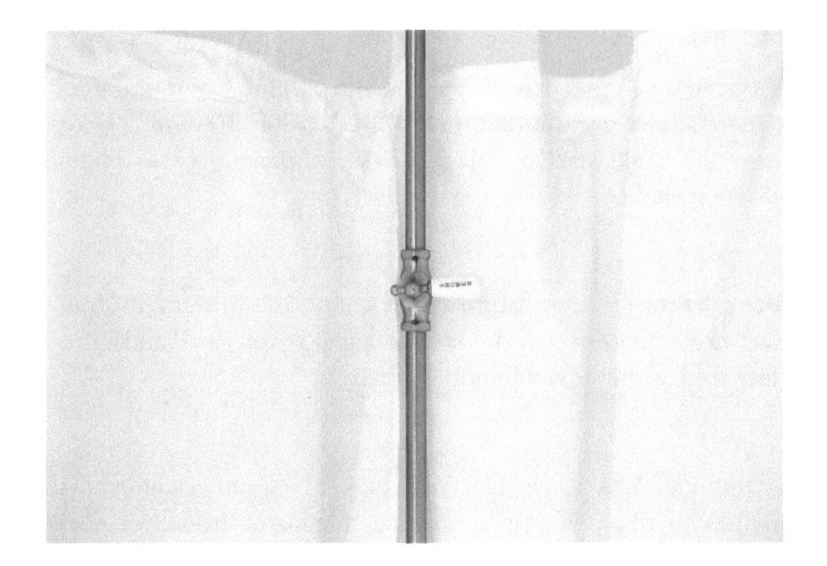

Designing and Installing Effective Venting Systems: Optimize Your Plumbing and Enhance Indoor Air Quality

PROPER VENTING IS crucial for the efficient operation of your plumbing system and maintaining good indoor air quality. In this section, we'll guide you through the process of designing and installing effective venting systems, ensuring your plumbing performs optimally and your home remains comfortable and healthy.

Understanding Venting Basics

VENTING systems equalize air pressure within your plumbing system, allowing wastewater to flow freely while preventing sewer gases from entering your home. Key components of a venting system include:

VENT STACK: A vertical pipe that connects to the main drain line, extending through the roof to expel sewer gases and introduce fresh air into the plumbing system.

INDIVIDUAL VENTS: Smaller vent pipes that connect individual fixtures to the vent stack, ensuring adequate airflow for each plumbing fixture.

WET VENTING: A combined drain and vent system where one pipe serves both as a drain for one fixture and a vent for another.

Designing the Venting System

Before starting the installation, design your venting system according to local building codes and best practices. Consider the following aspects:

FIXTURE UNITS AND PIPE SIZES: Determine the total number of fixture units in your plumbing system and the appropriate pipe sizes for the vent stack and individual vents based on fixture unit values.

VENT CONNECTIONS: Design your venting system to ensure all plumbing fixtures are properly connected to the vent stack or individual vents, minimizing the risk of sewer gas infiltration and maintaining optimal airflow.

VENT DISTANCES: Ensure that vent connections are within the allowable distance from the plumbing fixtures, as specified by local building codes, to maintain proper airflow and prevent siphoning of water in fixture traps.

Preparing for Installation

ONCE THE DESIGN IS FINALIZED, gather the necessary tools and materials, such as PVC or ABS pipes, fittings, primer, and cement. Review local building codes to ensure compliance and obtain any necessary permits.

Installing the Venting System

FOLLOW these steps to install your venting system, ensuring secure connections and proper slope for optimal performance:

. . .

Vent Stack Installation: Connect the vent stack to the main drain line and run it vertically through your home, extending it above the roofline. Ensure the vent stack maintains a consistent slope (1/4 inch per foot) and has no horizontal sections.

Individual Vent Installation: Connect each plumbing fixture to the vent stack or individual vents using appropriately sized pipes and fittings. Ensure that the vents maintain a consistent slope (1/4 inch per foot) and have no horizontal sections. If using wet venting, verify that the combined drain and vent system meets local building code requirements.

Roof Penetration: Cut a hole in the roof for the vent stack, ensuring a watertight seal with appropriate flashing and roofing materials. Extend the vent stack at least 6 inches above the roofline to prevent the entry of debris or precipitation.

Testing and Fine-tuning

Once the venting system is installed, test your plumbing system for proper operation. Run water through all fixtures and observe the drainage, checking for any signs of slow draining or sewer gas odors. Make any necessary adjustments to the venting system to optimize performance.

Finishing Touches

Seal any wall or ceiling penetrations created during the venting system installation with appropriate fire-resistant materials, caulk, or sealant.

. . .

CONGRATULATIONS! By designing and installing an effective venting system, you've optimized your plumbing performance and enhanced indoor air quality in your home. Enjoy the benefits of a well-functioning plumbing system and take pride in your impressive DIY accomplishment!

Addressing Complex Drainage Challenges: Expert Solutions for Optimal Plumbing Performance

COMPLEX DRAINAGE CHALLENGES can arise in various situations, such as remodeling projects, unique architectural designs, or difficult terrain. In this section, we'll guide you through addressing complex drainage challenges, ensuring your plumbing system performs optimally and efficiently.

Identifying Drainage Challenges

START by identifying the unique challenges that your plumbing system may face. Common complex drainage challenges include:

LIMITED SPACE: Constrained areas or non-standard layouts can create challenges in designing and installing an efficient drainage system.

MULTIPLE LEVELS OR SPLIT-LEVEL HOMES: A multi-level or split-level home may require additional consideration for proper drainage and venting.

TERRAIN AND SLOPE: Homes built on slopes, hills, or uneven terrain may experience drainage challenges due to the increased risk of water backflow, flooding, or erosion.

Developing a Comprehensive Plan

Advanced Plumbing Techniques

ONCE YOU HAVE IDENTIFIED the specific challenges, develop a comprehensive plan to address them, considering the following aspects:

PROPER SLOPE AND DRAINAGE: Ensure that the drainage system maintains the appropriate slope (typically 1/4 inch per foot) to promote the free flow of wastewater.

VENTING MODIFICATIONS: Incorporate necessary venting modifications, such as loop vents, island vents, or air admittance valves, to maintain proper airflow and prevent sewer gas infiltration.

SUMP PUMPS AND BACKWATER VALVES: For homes prone to flooding or backflow issues, consider installing sump pumps and backwater valves to protect against water damage and sewage backups.

FRENCH DRAINS AND DRAINAGE SWALES: Address outdoor drainage challenges by incorporating French drains or drainage swales to redirect excess water away from your home's foundation.

Consulting with Professionals

FOR COMPLEX DRAINAGE CHALLENGES, it is often best to consult with professionals, such as plumbers, architects, or civil engineers, to ensure that your drainage system adheres to local building codes and best practices.

Implementing the Plan

Once your comprehensive plan has been developed and approved, gather the necessary tools and materials for the project. Obtain any required permits and coordinate with professionals as needed.

Testing and Fine-tuning

After implementing your plan, test the drainage system for proper operation. Run water through all fixtures and observe the drainage, checking for any signs of slow draining, backflow, or sewer gas odors. Make any necessary adjustments to optimize the system's performance.

Maintenance and Monitoring

Regularly maintain and monitor your drainage system to ensure its continued efficiency. Clear debris from outdoor drains, clean and inspect sump pumps, and check for signs of wear or damage.

By addressing complex drainage challenges, you can ensure that your plumbing system operates efficiently and effectively in even the most demanding situations. With careful planning and the help of professionals, you can overcome these challenges and enjoy the benefits of a well-functioning plumbing system.

Installing and Maintaining Backflow Prevention Devices: Safeguard Your Water Supply and Ensure Public Health

BACKFLOW PREVENTION DEVICES are essential for protecting your water supply from contamination due to backflow, ensuring the safety and health of your household and community. In this section, we'll guide you through the process of installing and maintaining backflow prevention devices, providing a crucial safeguard for your water supply.

Understanding Backflow and Its Causes

BACKFLOW OCCURS when water from your plumbing system flows back into the public water supply, potentially contaminating it with pollutants or contaminants. Common causes of backflow include:

BACKPRESSURE: Increased pressure in your plumbing system can force water to flow in the opposite direction, resulting in backflow.

BACKSIPHONAGE: A sudden drop in water pressure, such as during a water main break or heavy water usage, can create a vacuum effect, drawing water back into the public water supply.

Selecting the Appropriate Backflow Prevention Device

CHOOSE the right backflow prevention device for your specific needs and local regulations. Common types include:

. . .

AIR GAP: A physical separation between the water supply and a plumbing fixture, ensuring that no direct connection exists for contaminants to enter the water supply.

ATMOSPHERIC VACUUM BREAKER (AVB): A device that prevents backsiphonage by closing a valve when water pressure drops, stopping the flow of water.

PRESSURE VACUUM BREAKER (PVB): Similar to an AVB, a PVB also prevents backpressure-induced backflow by closing a valve when water pressure increases.

REDUCED PRESSURE ZONE (RPZ) ASSEMBLY: A complex device that uses a combination of check valves and pressure relief valves to prevent both backpressure and backsiphonage.

Installing the Backflow Prevention Device

FOLLOW these general steps to install your chosen backflow prevention device, ensuring secure connections and proper operation:

1. Turn off the water supply and release pressure from the system by opening a faucet.
2. Install the backflow prevention device according to the manufacturer's instructions and local building codes. This may involve connecting the device to your water main, irrigation system, or specific plumbing fixtures.
3. Ensure proper orientation and installation height, as specified by the manufacturer and local regulations.

4. Turn the water supply back on and test the device for proper operation, checking for leaks and correct water flow direction.

Maintaining Your Backflow Prevention Device

REGULAR MAINTENANCE IS essential to ensure the continued effectiveness of your backflow prevention device. Follow these general maintenance guidelines:

INSPECTION: Inspect the device regularly for signs of wear, damage, or malfunction. Some devices may require annual inspections by certified professionals to comply with local regulations.

TESTING: Test your backflow prevention device periodically, as recommended by the manufacturer and local regulations. This may involve hiring a certified backflow tester to ensure proper operation and compliance.

CLEANING AND REPAIR: Clean and repair your backflow prevention device as needed, following the manufacturer's guidelines. Replace worn or damaged parts promptly to maintain optimal performance.

BY INSTALLING and maintaining backflow prevention devices, you are safeguarding your water supply and ensuring the health and safety of your household and community. With proper care and attention, these devices provide an essential layer of protection for your water system.

Properly Sizing and Locating Cleanouts: Streamline Maintenance and Avoid Plumbing Issues

CLEANOUTS ARE essential components of your plumbing system, providing easy access for maintenance and clearing blockages. In this section, we'll guide you through the process of properly sizing and locating cleanouts, ensuring efficient maintenance and reduced risk of plumbing issues.

Understanding Cleanouts

CLEANOUTS ARE openings in your plumbing system's drain and sewer lines, covered by removable caps or plugs. They provide access for inspection, cleaning, and removal of blockages, making them crucial for maintaining your plumbing system's performance.

Sizing Cleanouts

SELECTING the appropriate size for your cleanouts is essential for ensuring easy access and effective maintenance. Follow these guidelines:

MATCH CLEANOUT SIZE to Pipe Diameter: Cleanouts should generally match the diameter of the pipe they serve, with a minimum size of 2 inches for residential applications and 3 inches for commercial applications.

. . .

Advanced Plumbing Techniques

ACCESSIBILITY: Ensure that the cleanout size allows for easy access and the use of standard plumbing tools, such as snakes or augers, for clearing blockages.

Locating Cleanouts

PROPER CLEANOUT PLACEMENT is critical for efficient maintenance and quick resolution of plumbing issues. Consider the following aspects when determining cleanout locations:

BUILDING CODES: Consult local building codes for specific requirements regarding cleanout placement, including minimum and maximum distances from fixtures, changes in direction, and pipe size.

ACCESSIBLE LOCATIONS: Place cleanouts in easily accessible locations, avoiding obstructed or concealed areas that could hinder maintenance efforts.

HORIZONTAL DRAIN LINES: Install cleanouts at the base of vertical stacks and at regular intervals along horizontal drain lines, typically every 50 to 100 feet for residential applications and every 100 feet for commercial applications.

CHANGES IN DIRECTION: Place cleanouts near changes in direction, such as bends or junctions, where blockages are more likely to occur. Install cleanouts on both sides of 90-degree bends and at least one cleanout for every 135-degree change in direction.

. . .

BUILDING PERIMETER: Install cleanouts near the building's perimeter, providing access to the main sewer line and facilitating maintenance of the building's exterior plumbing system.

Installing Cleanouts

FOLLOW these general steps to install your cleanouts, ensuring secure connections and proper function:

1. Turn off the water supply and release pressure from the system by opening a faucet.
2. Cut the appropriate-sized hole in the drain or sewer line at the chosen location, ensuring a snug fit for the cleanout fitting.
3. Install the cleanout fitting using the appropriate adhesive or sealant, following the manufacturer's instructions and local building codes.
4. Attach the cleanout cap or plug, ensuring a watertight seal.
5. Turn the water supply back on and test the plumbing system for proper operation, checking for leaks around the cleanout fitting.

BY PROPERLY SIZING and locating cleanouts, you streamline maintenance efforts and minimize the risk of plumbing issues in your home or building. With thoughtful planning and adherence to local building codes, you can ensure easy access to your plumbing system for efficient inspection, cleaning, and blockage removal.

complex water supply system repairs and installations
. . .

Working with Pressure Reducing Valves: Optimize Water Pressure and Enhance Plumbing System Performance

PRESSURE REDUCING valves (PRVs) are essential components of a plumbing system that help maintain optimal water pressure, preventing issues like water hammer, leaks, and appliance damage. In this section, we'll guide you through working with pressure reducing valves, ensuring your plumbing system performs efficiently and effectively.

Understanding Pressure Reducing Valves

A PRESSURE REDUCING valve is a device that automatically reduces the incoming water pressure to a desired, stable level. PRVs protect your plumbing system and appliances from high water pressure, which can cause leaks, pipe damage, and reduced appliance lifespan.

Selecting the Appropriate PRV

CHOOSE the right PRV for your specific needs and local regulations. Consider the following aspects:

PRESSURE RANGE: Select a PRV with an adjustable pressure range suitable for your home or building's requirements. Typical residential water pressure ranges from 40 to 60 psi, while commercial applications may require higher pressures.

CONNECTION SIZE: Ensure the PRV's connection size matches the size of your main water supply pipe.

Flow Rate: Choose a PRV with a flow rate capacity that meets or exceeds your plumbing system's maximum demand.

Material Compatibility: Select a PRV made from materials compatible with your plumbing system, such as brass or stainless steel, to ensure durability and prevent corrosion.

Installing the Pressure Reducing Valve

Follow these general steps to install your PRV, ensuring secure connections and proper operation:

1. Turn off the main water supply and release pressure from the system by opening a faucet.
2. Locate an appropriate installation point, typically on the main water line after the water meter and shut-off valve.
3. Cut the pipe at the chosen location, ensuring a clean, square cut.
4. Install the PRV according to the manufacturer's instructions and local building codes, ensuring proper orientation and allowing for expansion and contraction of the pipe.
5. Turn the main water supply back on and adjust the PRV to the desired pressure, following the manufacturer's guidelines.
6. Test the plumbing system for proper operation, checking for leaks around the PRV connections and verifying the desired water pressure.

Maintaining Your Pressure Reducing Valve

REGULAR MAINTENANCE IS essential to ensure the continued effectiveness of your PRV. Follow these general maintenance guidelines:

INSPECTION: Inspect the PRV regularly for signs of wear, damage, or malfunction, such as unusual noises or fluctuating water pressure.

CLEANING: Clean the PRV's internal components, such as the strainer or diaphragm, as needed to remove debris and maintain optimal performance.

REPLACEMENT: Replace worn or damaged parts, such as O-rings, gaskets, or diaphragms, promptly to ensure proper function. If necessary, replace the entire PRV according to the manufacturer's recommended service life.

BY WORKING with pressure reducing valves, you can optimize water pressure in your home or building, enhancing the performance of your plumbing system and protecting it from potential damage. With proper selection, installation, and maintenance, PRVs provide a valuable safeguard for your plumbing system and appliances.

Advanced Plumbing Techniques

Installing Booster Pumps and Water Storage Tanks: Enhance Water Pressure and Ensure Consistent Supply

BOOSTER PUMPS and water storage tanks are valuable additions to a plumbing system, improving water pressure and providing a consistent supply during periods of high demand or low water pressure. In this section, we'll guide you through the process of installing booster pumps and water storage tanks, ensuring optimal performance and reliability.

Understanding Booster Pumps and Water Storage Tanks

A BOOSTER PUMP is a device that increases water pressure in your plumbing system, enhancing the performance of fixtures and appliances. Water storage tanks provide a reserve of water, ensuring a consistent supply during periods of high demand or low pressure from the main water source.

Selecting the Appropriate Booster Pump

CHOOSE the right booster pump for your specific needs, considering the following aspects:

PRESSURE BOOST: Select a booster pump with a pressure boost sufficient to meet your home or building's requirements, taking into account factors like the number of fixtures and the desired flow rate.

. . .

FLOW RATE CAPACITY: Choose a booster pump with a flow rate capacity that meets or exceeds your plumbing system's maximum demand.

POWER SOURCE: Ensure the booster pump's power source, whether electric or gas-powered, is compatible with your home or building's available power supply.

Selecting the Appropriate Water Storage Tank

CHOOSE the right water storage tank for your specific needs, considering the following aspects:

MATERIAL: Select a water storage tank made from materials compatible with your water supply and local regulations, such as polyethylene, fiberglass, or steel.

CAPACITY: Choose a water storage tank with a capacity sufficient to meet your home or building's water demand during periods of peak usage or low water pressure.

SPACE AND LOCATION: Ensure the selected water storage tank fits within the available space and is suitable for the intended installation location, whether indoor, outdoor, above ground, or below ground.

Installing the Booster Pump and Water Storage Tank

Advanced Plumbing Techniques

Follow these general steps to install your booster pump and water storage tank, ensuring secure connections and proper operation:

1. Turn off the main water supply and release pressure from the system by opening a faucet.
2. Install the water storage tank according to the manufacturer's instructions and local building codes, ensuring proper support and a secure connection to the plumbing system.
3. Install the booster pump according to the manufacturer's instructions, typically on the main water line between the storage tank and the home or building's plumbing system.
4. Ensure proper electrical or gas connections for the booster pump, following the manufacturer's guidelines and local building codes.
5. Turn the main water supply back on and adjust the booster pump to the desired pressure, following the manufacturer's guidelines.
6. Test the plumbing system for proper operation, checking for leaks around the booster pump and storage tank connections and verifying the desired water pressure.

Maintaining Your Booster Pump and Water Storage Tank

Regular maintenance is essential to ensure the continued effectiveness of your booster pump and water storage tank. Follow these general maintenance guidelines:

. . .

INSPECTION: Inspect the booster pump and water storage tank regularly for signs of wear, damage, or malfunction, such as unusual noises, leaks, or fluctuating water pressure.

CLEANING AND FLUSHING: Clean and flush the water storage tank periodically to remove sediment and prevent bacterial growth. Follow the manufacturer's guidelines for proper cleaning procedures.

LUBRICATION AND PARTS REPLACEMENT: Lubricate moving parts of the booster pump, as needed, and replace worn or damaged parts, such as seals or bearings, to ensure optimal performance and a long service life.

BY INSTALLING booster pumps and water storage tanks, you can enhance water pressure and ensure a consistent water supply in your home or building. With proper selection, installation, and maintenance, these components provide reliable

Advanced Techniques for Fixing Water Hammer Issues: Protect Your Plumbing System and Minimize Noise

WATER HAMMER IS a common plumbing issue characterized by loud banging or knocking sounds in pipes, often caused by a sudden stop or change in water flow. In this section, we'll cover advanced techniques for fixing water hammer issues, protecting your plumbing system from potential damage and minimizing disruptive noise.

Understanding Water Hammer

WATER HAMMER OCCURS when water suddenly changes direction or stops flowing, causing a pressure wave that travels through the plumbing system. This pressure wave can cause pipes to vibrate, resulting in the characteristic banging or knocking sound. Prolonged water hammer issues can lead to pipe damage, leaks, and reduced appliance lifespan.

Installing Water Hammer Arrestors

WATER HAMMER ARRESTORS are devices designed to absorb the pressure wave caused by water hammer, protecting your plumbing system from damage. Install water hammer arrestors at strategic locations in your plumbing system, such as near appliances, fixtures, or valves prone to causing water hammer. Follow the manufacturer's guidelines and local building codes for proper installation and sizing.

Upgrading to Slow-Closing Valves

SLOW-CLOSING VALVES HELP to minimize water hammer by gradually reducing water flow, preventing sudden stops that cause pressure surges. Consider upgrading to slow-closing valves on fixtures and appliances that are prone to causing water hammer issues, such as washing machines, dishwashers, and toilets.

Balancing Your Plumbing System

AN UNBALANCED PLUMBING system can contribute to water hammer issues. Ensure proper balancing by adjusting individual fixture flow rates, checking for proper pipe sizing, and maintaining consistent water pressure throughout the system. Consult with a professional plumber if you're unsure how to properly balance your plumbing system.

Insulating and Securing Pipes

LOOSE OR IMPROPERLY SECURED pipes can exacerbate water hammer issues by allowing excessive movement and vibration. Inspect your plumbing system and ensure all pipes are properly secured with appropriate brackets, hangers, or strapping. Additionally, insulate pipes to minimize noise transmission and further stabilize the system.

Installing Pressure Reducing Valves (PRVs)

HIGH WATER PRESSURE can contribute to water hammer issues. If your water pressure exceeds the recommended range (typically 40 to 60 psi for residential applications), consider installing a pressure reducing valve to maintain a consistent, lower pressure level throughout your plumbing system.

Regular Maintenance and Inspection

Advanced Plumbing Techniques

REGULARLY INSPECT your plumbing system for signs of wear, damage, or loose connections that could contribute to water hammer issues. Perform maintenance tasks, such as cleaning aerators, flushing water heaters, and testing pressure relief valves, to ensure optimal system performance and minimize the risk of water hammer problems.

BY IMPLEMENTING these advanced techniques for fixing water hammer issues, you can protect your plumbing system from potential damage, minimize noise, and enhance the overall performance of your plumbing system. With proper maintenance and proactive measures, you can prevent water hammer and ensure the longevity of your pipes and fixtures.

Installing and Repairing Water Filtration Systems: Improve Water Quality and Safeguard Your Health

WATER FILTRATION SYSTEMS are essential for ensuring clean, safe drinking water in your home or building. In this section, we'll guide you through installing and repairing water filtration systems, helping you improve water quality and protect your health.

Understanding Water Filtration Systems

WATER FILTRATION SYSTEMS REMOVE IMPURITIES, such as sediment, chlorine, heavy metals, and harmful contaminants, from your water supply. These systems can include whole-house filters, under-sink filters, and countertop filters, depending on your specific needs and preferences.

Selecting the Appropriate Water Filtration System

CHOOSE the right water filtration system for your specific needs, considering the following aspects:

CONTAMINANTS: Select a water filtration system designed to remove the specific contaminants present in your water supply. You may need to perform a water test or consult your local water utility for this information.

. . .

Advanced Plumbing Techniques

FLOW RATE: Choose a water filtration system with a flow rate capacity that meets or exceeds your plumbing system's maximum demand.

FILTER TYPE: Select a water filtration system with the appropriate filter type, such as activated carbon, reverse osmosis, or ultraviolet disinfection, based on your water quality and desired level of filtration.

Installing a Water Filtration System

FOLLOW these general steps to install your water filtration system, ensuring secure connections and proper operation:

1. Turn off the main water supply and release pressure from the system by opening a faucet.
2. Install the water filtration system according to the manufacturer's instructions and local building codes, ensuring proper support and a secure connection to the plumbing system.
3. Install the filter cartridge, following the manufacturer's guidelines for proper orientation and seating.
4. Turn the main water supply back on and flush the water filtration system, as directed by the manufacturer, to remove any air or debris.
5. Test the plumbing system for proper operation, checking for leaks around the water filtration system connections and verifying the desired water quality.

Repairing a Water Filtration System

If your water filtration system is not functioning correctly or showing signs of wear, follow these general steps to diagnose and repair the issue:

1. Inspect the system for signs of damage, leaks, or clogs, such as reduced water flow or an unusual taste or odor.
2. Check the filter cartridge for blockages, wear, or damage, and replace it as needed, following the manufacturer's guidelines for proper installation and filter life.
3. Inspect the plumbing connections and fittings for leaks or damage, tightening or replacing them as necessary.
4. Consult the manufacturer's troubleshooting guide or contact a professional plumber if you're unable to identify or resolve the issue.

Maintaining Your Water Filtration System

REGULAR MAINTENANCE IS essential to ensure the continued effectiveness of your water filtration system. Follow these general maintenance guidelines:

REPLACE FILTER CARTRIDGES: Regularly replace the filter cartridges according to the manufacturer's recommendations and your specific water usage patterns to maintain optimal filtration performance.

CLEAN THE SYSTEM: Periodically clean the water filtration system, including the filter housing and any components prone to sediment buildup, following the manufacturer's guidelines for proper cleaning procedures.

MONITOR WATER QUALITY: Regularly test your water quality to ensure the filtration system is effectively removing contaminants and maintaining the desired level of purity.

BY INSTALLING and repairing water filtration systems, you can improve water quality in your home or building, safeguarding your health and enhancing the taste and clarity of your water supply. With proper selection, installation, and maintenance, water filtration systems provide a reliable solution for clean, safe drinking water.

advanced troubleshooting and problem-solving
. . .

Diagnosing and Repairing Complex Leaks: Safeguard Your Property and Save on Water Bills

COMPLEX LEAKS CAN CAUSE significant damage to your property and result in increased water bills. In this section, we'll guide you through diagnosing and repairing complex leaks, helping you protect your property and save on water expenses.

Identifying the Presence of Complex Leaks

COMPLEX LEAKS CAN BE HIDDEN within walls, floors, or ceilings and may not be immediately apparent. Signs of complex leaks can include:

- Unexplained increases in water bills
- Dampness, mold, or mildew on walls, ceilings, or floors
- Warped or stained surfaces
- Unusual sounds, such as dripping or running water when fixtures are not in use

Locating Complex Leaks

LOCATING complex leaks can be challenging, as they may be hidden or difficult to access. Use these techniques to help locate complex leaks:

VISUAL INSPECTION: Carefully inspect your property for signs of water damage, dampness, or mold, paying particular attention to areas near plumbing fixtures or pipes.

. . .

Advanced Plumbing Techniques

MOISTURE METER: Use a moisture meter to measure the moisture content of walls, ceilings, and floors, looking for unusual or elevated readings that may indicate a hidden leak.

ACOUSTIC LEAK DETECTION: Employ acoustic leak detection equipment, such as listening devices or ground microphones, to listen for the sound of running water or dripping within walls, floors, or ceilings.

INFRARED THERMOGRAPHY: Utilize infrared thermography cameras to identify temperature differences that may indicate the presence of a hidden leak, as wet areas typically have a different temperature compared to dry areas.

PROFESSIONAL ASSISTANCE: Consult a professional plumber or leak detection specialist if you're unable to locate the leak using these techniques.

Repairing Complex Leaks

ONCE YOU'VE LOCATED a complex leak, follow these steps to repair it and prevent further damage:

1. Turn off the main water supply and release pressure from the system by opening a faucet.
2. Access the leak by carefully removing any obstacles, such as drywall or flooring, taking care to minimize damage to your property.
3. Inspect the affected area and determine the cause of the leak, such as a damaged pipe, loose fitting, or corroded valve.

4. Repair the leak by replacing damaged components, tightening loose connections, or applying appropriate sealants, ensuring a secure and watertight connection.
5. Test the plumbing system for proper operation, checking for leaks around the repaired area and verifying the issue has been resolved.
6. Restore the affected area by replacing any removed materials and repairing any damage caused during the leak detection and repair process.

Preventing Future Complex Leaks

PREVENT future complex leaks by implementing these proactive measures:

REGULAR INSPECTION: Regularly inspect your plumbing system for signs of wear, damage, or loose connections that could lead to leaks, and perform necessary maintenance tasks.

PROPER INSTALLATION: Ensure all plumbing components are installed correctly and follow local building codes to minimize the risk of leaks.

WATER PRESSURE MANAGEMENT: Maintain a consistent, appropriate water pressure level (typically 40 to 60 psi for residential applications) to reduce stress on pipes and fittings.

PIPE INSULATION: Insulate pipes exposed to temperature fluctuations or extreme conditions to prevent damage and leaks due to freezing or expansion.

. . .

BY DIAGNOSING and repairing complex leaks, you can protect your property from water damage and save on water bills. With proper detection techniques, timely repairs, and proactive prevention measures, you can minimize the risk of complex leaks and maintain the integrity of your plumbing system.

Solving Persistent Clogs and Blockages: Keep Your Plumbing System Flowing Smoothly and Avoid Unwanted Disruptions

PERSISTENT CLOGS and blockages can cause significant inconvenience and disrupt the normal functioning of your plumbing system. In this section, we'll guide you through solving persistent clogs and blockages, helping you maintain a smooth-flowing plumbing system and avoid unwanted disruptions.

Identifying Persistent Clogs and Blockages

PERSISTENT CLOGS and blockages are characterized by recurring or continuous slow draining or backed-up water in your plumbing fixtures, such as sinks, toilets, and bathtubs. These issues can be caused by a variety of factors, including:

- Accumulation of debris or foreign objects
- Buildup of grease, hair, or soap scum
- Tree root intrusion in underground pipes
- Structural issues, such as pipe sagging or misalignment

Clearing Common Clogs and Blockages

BEFORE ADDRESSING PERSISTENT CLOGS, try these basic methods to clear common clogs and blockages:

PLUNGER: Use a plunger to create suction and dislodge the clog, ensuring a proper seal and applying consistent pressure.

CHEMICAL DRAIN CLEANER: Apply a chemical drain cleaner, following the manufacturer's guidelines for proper usage and safety precautions.

MANUAL OR HANDHELD AUGER: Use a manual or handheld auger (also known as a plumber's snake) to reach and break up clogs within your pipes.

HIGH-PRESSURE WATER JETTING: Employ high-pressure water jetting equipment to blast away stubborn clogs and debris, ensuring the appropriate pressure level is used to prevent pipe damage.

Diagnosing Persistent Clogs and Blockages

IF BASIC METHODS fail to resolve the issue, take these steps to diagnose the cause of persistent clogs and blockages:

1. Perform a visual inspection of accessible pipes and fixtures, looking for signs of damage or obstruction.
2. Use a plumbing camera to inspect the interior of your pipes, identifying the location and nature of the clog or blockage.
3. Consult a professional plumber if you're unable to diagnose the issue or require specialized equipment for further investigation.

Addressing the Root Cause of Persistent Clogs and Blockages

ONCE THE CAUSE of the persistent clog or blockage has been identified, take the appropriate steps to resolve the issue:

REMOVE FOREIGN OBJECTS: Carefully remove any foreign objects lodged within your pipes, using specialized retrieval tools or professional assistance as needed.

CLEAR GREASE, Hair, or Soap Scum Buildup: Use enzyme-based drain cleaners or professional cleaning services to break down and remove stubborn buildup from your pipes.

ADDRESS TREE ROOT INTRUSION: Employ professional root removal services or chemical treatments to clear tree roots from your underground pipes, and take preventative measures, such as root barriers, to prevent future intrusion.

REPAIR STRUCTURAL ISSUES: Consult a professional plumber to repair or replace damaged, sagging, or misaligned pipes, ensuring a proper slope and alignment for optimal flow.

Preventing Future Persistent Clogs and Blockages

IMPLEMENT these preventive measures to minimize the risk of future persistent clogs and blockages:

REGULAR MAINTENANCE: Regularly clean and maintain your plumbing system, including drain cleaning, pipe inspections, and the removal of debris from traps and screens.

. . .

PROPER DISPOSAL PRACTICES: Avoid disposing of grease, oil, or non-biodegradable items down your drains, and use drain screens to catch hair, food particles, and other debris.

PLUMBING SYSTEM UPGRADES: Consider upgrading to larger pipes, installing backwater valves, or implementing other plumbing system improvements to enhance flow and reduce the risk of clogs and blockages.

By solving persistent clogs and blockages, you can maintain a smooth-flowing plumbing system and avoid unwanted disruptions. With proper identification, diagnosis, and resolution of the root causes, along with proactive prevention measures, you can keep your plumbing system functioning optimally and minimize the risk of future clogs and blockages.

Tackling Advanced Sewer and Septic System Issues: Protect Your Property and the Environment

ADVANCED SEWER and septic system issues can pose a risk to your property and the environment. In this section, we'll guide you through tackling advanced sewer and septic system issues, helping you maintain a functional waste management system and protect your surroundings.

Identifying Advanced Sewer and Septic System Issues

ADVANCED SEWER and septic system issues can manifest in various ways, including:

- Sewage backups or slow drains
- Unpleasant odors around your property
- Soggy or flooded areas near the septic system or sewer lines
- Gurgling sounds from drains or toilets

Diagnosing Advanced Sewer and Septic System Issues

To DIAGNOSE the cause of advanced sewer and septic system issues, consider the following steps:

VISUAL INSPECTION: Inspect accessible sewer lines, septic tanks, and drain fields for signs of damage, leakage, or other issues.

Advanced Plumbing Techniques

. . .

Sewer Camera Inspection: Use a sewer camera to inspect the interior of your sewer lines, identifying blockages, damage, or other issues that may be causing the problem.

Septic System Inspection: Hire a professional septic system inspector to examine your septic tank, drain field, and other components for signs of malfunction or failure.

Professional Assistance: Consult a professional plumber or septic system specialist if you're unable to diagnose the issue using these techniques.

Addressing Advanced Sewer and Septic System Issues

Once the cause of the issue has been identified, take appropriate steps to address the problem:

Clear Blockages: Remove blockages from sewer lines using professional equipment, such as high-pressure water jetting or mechanical augers.

Repair or Replace Damaged Sewer Lines: Consult a professional plumber to repair or replace damaged sewer lines, ensuring proper installation and alignment for optimal flow.

Septic Tank Pumping and Cleaning: Have your septic tank pumped and cleaned by a professional septic service provider to remove sludge and restore its capacity.

REPAIR OR REPLACE **Septic System Components:** Hire a professional septic system contractor to repair or replace damaged or malfunctioning septic system components, such as the drain field, distribution box, or septic tank.

Preventing Future Advanced Sewer and Septic System Issues

IMPLEMENT these preventive measures to minimize the risk of future advanced sewer and septic system issues:

REGULAR MAINTENANCE: Schedule regular sewer line and septic system inspections, cleanings, and maintenance to ensure proper functioning and prevent potential issues.

PROPER DISPOSAL PRACTICES: Avoid disposing of grease, oil, or non-biodegradable items down your drains, and use septic-safe products to minimize the risk of blockages or system failure.

TREE ROOT MANAGEMENT: Protect your sewer lines and septic system from tree root intrusion by planting trees and shrubs at a safe distance and installing root barriers if necessary.

WATER CONSERVATION: Conserve water by using high-efficiency plumbing fixtures and appliances, reducing the burden on your septic system and minimizing the risk of overloading or failure.

BY TACKLING advanced sewer and septic system issues, you can protect your property and the environment from the consequences of malfunctioning waste management systems. With proper diagnosis, resolution, and prevention measures, you can maintain a functional and efficient sewer or septic system and minimize the risk of future issues.

Addressing Water Pressure and Temperature Inconsistencies: Ensure Comfort and Functionality in Your Home

WATER PRESSURE and temperature inconsistencies can be frustrating and affect the comfort and functionality of your home. In this section, we'll guide you through addressing these issues, helping you achieve consistent water pressure and temperature throughout your property.

Identifying Water Pressure and Temperature Inconsistencies

COMMON SIGNS of water pressure and temperature inconsistencies include:

- Fluctuating water pressure when using multiple fixtures simultaneously
- Sudden drops in water pressure or temperature when another fixture is used
- Inadequate hot water supply or inconsistent water temperature

Diagnosing Water Pressure and Temperature Inconsistencies

TO DIAGNOSE the cause of water pressure and temperature inconsistencies, consider the following steps:

Advanced Plumbing Techniques

INSPECT PLUMBING SYSTEM: Check for any visible signs of damage or wear in your plumbing system, such as leaks, corroded pipes, or faulty valves.

ASSESS WATER PRESSURE: Use a water pressure gauge to measure the water pressure at various fixtures throughout your home, noting any significant variations or inconsistencies.

EVALUATE WATER HEATER PERFORMANCE: Inspect your water heater for proper operation, including temperature settings, capacity, and heating elements.

PROFESSIONAL ASSISTANCE: Consult a professional plumber if you're unable to diagnose the issue using these techniques.

Addressing Water Pressure Inconsistencies

ONCE THE CAUSE of water pressure inconsistencies has been identified, take appropriate steps to address the problem:

REPAIR OR REPLACE DAMAGED PIPES: Consult a professional plumber to repair or replace damaged or corroded pipes, ensuring proper installation and alignment for optimal water flow.

CLEAN OR REPLACE FAUCET AERATORS: Remove, clean, or replace faucet aerators to remove debris and improve water flow.

INSTALL PRESSURE REGULATING VALVES: Install pressure regulating valves (PRVs) to maintain consistent water pressure throughout your home, adjusting the settings according to your desired pressure level.

UPGRADE PLUMBING SYSTEM: Consider upgrading to larger pipes, booster pumps, or other plumbing system improvements to enhance water pressure and flow.

Addressing Water Temperature Inconsistencies

ONCE THE CAUSE of water temperature inconsistencies has been identified, take appropriate steps to address the problem:

ADJUST WATER HEATER SETTINGS: Check and adjust your water heater temperature settings to ensure they are set at an appropriate level, typically between 120°F and 140°F.

INSPECT AND REPAIR Water Heater Components: Examine your water heater for damaged or malfunctioning components, such as heating elements or thermostats, and replace or repair them as needed.

FLUSH WATER HEATER TANK: Flush your water heater tank to remove sediment buildup, which can reduce heating efficiency and cause temperature fluctuations.

UPGRADE WATER HEATER: Consider upgrading to a larger capacity or more efficient water heater to better meet your household's hot water demands.

Preventing Future Water Pressure and Temperature Inconsistencies

IMPLEMENT these preventive measures to minimize the risk of future water pressure and temperature inconsistencies:

REGULAR MAINTENANCE: Schedule regular plumbing system and water heater inspections, cleanings, and maintenance to ensure proper functioning and prevent potential issues.

INSULATE PIPES: Insulate hot water pipes to maintain consistent water temperature as it travels through your plumbing system.

PROPER INSTALLATION: Ensure all plumbing components, including pipes, fixtures, and water heaters, are installed correctly and follow local building codes.

BY ADDRESSING water pressure and temperature inconsistencies, you can ensure comfort and functionality in your home. With proper diagnosis, resolution, and prevention measures, you can maintain a consistent and efficient plumbing system and minimize the risk of future issues.

plumbing for home additions and renovations
. . .

Planning and Designing Plumbing Systems for Home Additions: Enhance Your Living Space with a Seamless and Efficient Plumbing Integration

WHEN EXPANDING your living space with a home addition, planning and designing a well-integrated plumbing system is crucial. In this section, we'll guide you through the process of planning and designing plumbing systems for home additions, ensuring a seamless and efficient integration with your existing system.

Assessing Your Current Plumbing System

BEFORE STARTING THE DESIGN PROCESS, evaluate your current plumbing system to determine its capacity and compatibility with the proposed addition:

1. Examine the capacity of your water heater, septic system, and main water supply lines.
2. Inspect your existing plumbing system for any signs of damage, wear, or inadequate capacity.
3. Consult a professional plumber to assess your system and provide guidance on necessary upgrades or modifications.

Determining Plumbing Needs for the Home Addition

IDENTIFY the plumbing fixtures and components required for the home addition, considering:

Advanced Plumbing Techniques

- Bathroom fixtures, such as sinks, toilets, bathtubs, or showers.
- Kitchen fixtures, including sinks, dishwashers, or refrigerator water lines.
- Laundry room fixtures, such as washing machines and utility sinks.
- Outdoor plumbing needs, like hose bibs or irrigation systems.

Developing a Plumbing System Layout

CREATE a detailed plumbing system layout for the home addition, addressing the following factors:

FIXTURE LOCATIONS: Determine the optimal placement of plumbing fixtures, considering functionality, aesthetics, and space requirements.

PIPE ROUTING: Plan the most efficient and direct routes for supply lines, drain lines, and vent pipes, minimizing the risk of leaks or clogs.

PIPE SIZING: Ensure proper pipe sizing to accommodate the increased water flow and waste removal demands of the addition.

VENTING SYSTEM: Design an effective venting system to maintain proper air pressure, prevent sewer gases from entering your home, and comply with local building codes.

Selecting Plumbing Materials

CHOOSE appropriate materials for your plumbing system, considering factors such as durability, compatibility, and cost:

PIPES: Select pipe materials suitable for your needs, such as copper, PEX, PVC, CPVC, or ABS.

FIXTURES: Choose high-quality, water-efficient fixtures that match your home's style and meet your functional requirements.

VALVES AND FITTINGS: Opt for durable and reliable valves and fittings that are compatible with your chosen pipe materials.

Coordinating with Other Trades

COLLABORATE with other professionals involved in your home addition project, such as architects, electricians, and general contractors, to ensure a seamless integration of the plumbing system with other building components.

Obtaining Permits and Inspections

ENSURE compliance with local building codes and regulations by obtaining the necessary permits and scheduling required inspections during the construction process.

Hiring a Professional Plumber

HIRE a professional plumber with experience in home additions to oversee and execute the installation of the plumbing system, ensuring proper techniques, materials, and adherence to code requirements.

Post-Installation Maintenance

ONCE THE PLUMBING system has been installed, schedule regular maintenance, inspections, and repairs to keep it functioning optimally and prevent potential issues.

BY CAREFULLY PLANNING and designing the plumbing system for your home addition, you can ensure a seamless and efficient integration with your existing system. Collaborate with professionals, adhere to local building codes, and select appropriate materials to achieve a functional and attractive plumbing system that enhances your expanded living space.

Managing Complex Pipe Rerouting Projects: Ensuring a Successful and Efficient Plumbing Modification

COMPLEX PIPE REROUTING projects require careful planning, coordination, and execution to ensure a successful outcome. In this section, we'll guide you through managing complex pipe rerouting projects, helping you achieve an efficient and functional plumbing modification.

Assessing the Need for Pipe Rerouting

DETERMINE the reasons and requirements for pipe rerouting, considering factors such as:

- Home renovations or additions
- Repairing damaged or leaking pipes
- Improving water pressure or flow
- Updating outdated plumbing systems

Developing a Detailed Plan

CREATE a comprehensive plan for the pipe rerouting project, addressing the following elements:

EXISTING PLUMBING SYSTEM: Assess your current plumbing system, noting any limitations or issues that may impact the rerouting process.

. . .

REROUTING OBJECTIVES: Identify the specific goals of the pipe rerouting project, such as accommodating new fixtures, improving system efficiency, or addressing code violations.

PROPOSED LAYOUT: Design a new plumbing system layout that incorporates the rerouted pipes, ensuring efficient routing, proper pipe sizing, and effective venting.

MATERIAL SELECTION: Choose appropriate pipe materials for the rerouting project, considering durability, compatibility, and cost.

Coordinating with Other Trades

COLLABORATE with other professionals involved in your project, such as architects, electricians, and general contractors, to ensure a seamless integration of the rerouted plumbing system with other building components.

Obtaining Permits and Inspections

COMPLY WITH LOCAL building codes and regulations by obtaining necessary permits and scheduling required inspections during the rerouting process.

Hiring a Professional Plumber

ENGAGE a professional plumber with experience in complex pipe rerouting projects to oversee and execute the modifications, ensuring proper techniques, materials, and adherence to code requirements.

Preparing the Work Area

PREPARE the work area for pipe rerouting by:

1. Shutting off the water supply and draining the system
2. Protecting surrounding surfaces and structures from potential damage
3. Ensuring adequate lighting and ventilation in the work area

Executing the Pipe Rerouting

CARRY out the pipe rerouting project according to the detailed plan, following best practices for pipe installation and joining methods:

1. Safely remove or disconnect existing pipes that require rerouting.
2. Install new pipes according to the proposed layout, ensuring proper slope, support, and alignment.
3. Connect rerouted pipes to existing plumbing components, using appropriate joining methods and fittings.
4. Test the modified plumbing system for leaks and proper functionality.

Post-Project Maintenance

ONCE THE PIPE rerouting project has been completed, schedule regular maintenance, inspections, and repairs to keep the modified plumbing system functioning optimally and prevent potential issues.

By effectively managing complex pipe rerouting projects, you can achieve a successful and efficient plumbing modification that meets your objectives and complies with local building codes. Collaborate with professionals, adhere to best practices, and create a detailed plan to ensure a functional and well-integrated plumbing system that supports your home's needs.

Coordinating with Other Trades during Renovations: Ensuring a Smooth and Successful Project Collaboration

WHEN UNDERGOING A RENOVATION PROJECT, coordinating with various trades is essential to ensure a smooth and successful outcome. In this section, we'll guide you through the process of coordinating with other trades during renovations, helping you achieve an efficient and harmonious project collaboration.

Establishing Clear Communication Channels

EFFECTIVE COMMUNICATION IS crucial for successful collaboration. Establish clear communication channels among all trades involved, such as:

- Project meetings: Schedule regular project meetings to discuss progress, address issues, and share updates.
- Group communication tools: Utilize group communication tools, such as messaging apps, email threads, or project management software, to keep everyone informed and engaged.
- Contact information: Share contact information for all key personnel to facilitate easy communication between trades.

Developing a Comprehensive Project Plan

CREATE a detailed project plan that outlines the scope, timeline, and responsibilities of each trade involved. Ensure that the plan covers:

- Project milestones and deadlines
- Sequence of work for each trade
- Coordination requirements between trades
- Permits and inspections needed for each trade

Defining Roles and Responsibilities

CLEARLY DEFINE the roles and responsibilities of each trade to avoid confusion and conflicts. Ensure that everyone involved understands their duties and the expectations for their work.

Scheduling and Sequencing Work

ESTABLISH a coordinated work schedule that outlines the sequence of tasks for each trade, ensuring minimal disruption and efficient progress. Consider factors such as:

- Availability of trades
- Access to work areas
- Lead times for materials and equipment
- Dependencies between tasks

Coordinating On-Site Activities

MANAGE on-site activities to ensure smooth coordination between trades:

- Designate a site supervisor or project manager to oversee on-site activities and ensure that all trades follow the established schedule and plan.
- Ensure that each trade has adequate space, time, and access to perform their tasks without hindrance.
- Monitor the progress of each trade, addressing any issues or delays promptly to avoid project setbacks.

Sharing Resources and Information

ENCOURAGE collaboration and resource sharing among trades by:

- Sharing technical drawings, specifications, and other project documents
- Coordinating the delivery and storage of materials and equipment
- Sharing tools, equipment, or expertise when appropriate

Resolving Conflicts and Issues

ADDRESS ANY CONFLICTS or issues that arise during the project quickly and professionally, maintaining open communication and seeking compromise when necessary.

Conducting Post-Renovation Review

UPON COMPLETION of the renovation project, conduct a post-renovation review with all trades involved to discuss successes, challenges, and areas for improvement. This can help improve future collaborations and enhance the overall project experience.

Advanced Plumbing Techniques

...

BY EFFECTIVELY COORDINATING with other trades during renovations, you can ensure a smooth and successful project collaboration that meets your objectives and timelines. Establish clear communication channels, create a comprehensive project plan, and maintain strong on-site coordination to achieve an efficient and harmonious renovation project.

conclusion

...

Recap of advanced plumbing techniques covered

THIS CHAPTER IS DEVOTED to recapping the important information within the pages of this book as well as providing the next steps for those interested in applying what they learned in a professional capacity. Plumbing like many of the trades is a profession that is always in demand and the skills to do it successfully are more rare and valuable than ever!

IN THIS BOOK, we have covered various advanced plumbing techniques that can enhance your skills and help you tackle more complex projects. Here's a recap of the topics discussed:

- **Working with different pipe materials (Copper, PVC, CPVC, ABS): Understanding the unique properties, applications, and handling requirements for each pipe material.**

- **Pipe soldering and brazing techniques:** Mastering the art of joining copper pipes with soldering and brazing techniques for a watertight and long-lasting connection.
- **Pipe threading and joining methods:** Exploring various methods for threading and joining pipes, such as compression fittings, push-fit fittings, and threaded connections.
- **Installing luxury shower systems:** Learning how to design and install high-end shower systems, including multi-jet systems and rainfall showerheads.
- **Installing whirlpool tubs and spa baths:** Gaining expertise in the installation and maintenance of whirlpool tubs and spa baths for a luxurious bathing experience.
- **Integrating smart faucets and fixtures:** Familiarizing yourself with the latest in smart plumbing technology and incorporating these advanced fixtures into your projects.
- **Installing bidets and advanced toilet systems:** Expanding your skills to include the installation and maintenance of bidets and advanced toilet systems for increased comfort and functionality.
- **Designing and installing effective venting systems:** Understanding the importance of proper venting in plumbing systems and learning how to design and install effective venting solutions.
- **Addressing complex drainage challenges:** Acquiring the knowledge and skills to troubleshoot and resolve complex drainage issues.

- Installing and maintaining backflow prevention devices: Learning the importance of backflow prevention and mastering the installation and maintenance of these crucial devices.
- Properly sizing and locating cleanouts: Ensuring optimal performance of your plumbing system by correctly sizing and positioning cleanouts for easy maintenance access.
- Working with pressure reducing valves: Gaining expertise in the installation, adjustment, and maintenance of pressure reducing valves to optimize water pressure in your plumbing system.
- Installing booster pumps and water storage tanks: Enhancing your skills in the installation and maintenance of booster pumps and water storage tanks for improved water supply and pressure.
- Advanced techniques for fixing water hammer issues: Developing the skills to diagnose and address water hammer problems with various advanced solutions.
- Installing and repairing water filtration systems: Expanding your knowledge of water filtration systems and mastering their installation and repair.
- Diagnosing and repairing complex leaks: Enhancing your ability to identify and fix complex leaks in various plumbing systems.
- Solving persistent clogs and blockages: Acquiring the skills to tackle stubborn clogs and blockages in your plumbing system.
- Tackling advanced sewer and septic system issues: Gaining expertise in addressing

advanced sewer and septic system problems, ensuring efficient waste management.
- **Addressing water pressure and temperature inconsistencies:** Learning how to diagnose and resolve issues related to water pressure and temperature fluctuations in your plumbing system.
- **Planning and designing plumbing systems for home additions:** Mastering the process of planning and designing plumbing systems for home additions, ensuring seamless and efficient integration.
- **Managing complex pipe rerouting projects:** Enhancing your skills in managing and executing complex pipe rerouting projects for successful and efficient plumbing modifications.
- **Coordinating with other trades during renovations:** Learning the importance of collaboration and coordination with other trades during renovation projects for a smooth and successful outcome.

BY MASTERING these advanced plumbing techniques, you can take your plumbing skills to the next level, allowing you to tackle more complex projects and provide a higher level of service to your clients.

The Value of Continued Learning and Skill Development in the Plumbing Industry

Advanced Plumbing Techniques

CONTINUED LEARNING and skill development are essential for success in the plumbing industry. As technology advances and industry standards evolve, staying up-to-date with the latest techniques, materials, and best practices is crucial for maintaining a competitive edge. In this section, we'll discuss the value of continued learning and skill development for plumbing professionals.

STAYING COMPETITIVE IN THE INDUSTRY: By continually improving your skills and knowledge, you can set yourself apart from your competitors. This can lead to increased business opportunities, a better reputation, and a higher demand for your services.

MEETING INDUSTRY STANDARDS AND REGULATIONS: Building codes, industry standards, and regulations are constantly changing. Continued learning helps ensure that you stay current with these updates, avoiding costly mistakes, fines, or potential liabilities.

EXPANDING YOUR SERVICE OFFERINGS: As you develop new skills and learn about emerging technologies, you can expand your service offerings. This allows you to cater to a wider range of clients and projects, increasing your potential for revenue growth.

ENHANCING PROFESSIONALISM AND CREDIBILITY: Continued learning and skill development demonstrate your commitment to professionalism and quality workmanship. This can help you build credibility with clients, suppliers, and other industry professionals.

. . .

IMPROVING EFFICIENCY AND JOB PERFORMANCE: As you gain new skills and knowledge, you can become more efficient and effective in your work. This can lead to faster project completion times, reduced errors, and improved customer satisfaction.

FOSTERING A GROWTH MINDSET AND ADAPTABILITY: Embracing continued learning encourages a growth mindset and adaptability. This mindset can help you navigate changes in the industry, adapt to new technologies, and find innovative solutions to complex problems.

INCREASING Job Satisfaction and Career Growth: Investing in your professional development can lead to increased job satisfaction, as you gain confidence in your abilities and see the positive impact of your efforts. This can also open up new career opportunities, such as promotions, increased responsibility, or the ability to start your own business.

NETWORKING AND BUILDING PROFESSIONAL RELATIONSHIPS: Participating in industry events, workshops, and training programs can help you build valuable professional relationships with other industry professionals. Networking can lead to new business opportunities, collaborations, and valuable insights.

STAYING INFORMED about Emerging Trends and Technologies: Continued learning allows you to stay informed about emerging trends and technologies in the plumbing industry. This can help you make more informed decisions about the tools, materials, and techniques you use in your projects.

CONTRIBUTING to the Advancement of the Industry: By continually developing your skills and knowledge, you can contribute to the advancement of the plumbing industry. Sharing your expertise with others, participating in industry discussions, and adopting best practices can help improve the overall quality and professionalism of the industry.

IN CONCLUSION, the value of continued learning and skill development in the plumbing industry cannot be overstated. Investing in your professional growth can lead to increased competitiveness, improved job performance, and greater career satisfaction. By embracing a growth mindset and seeking opportunities for learning, you can ensure your long-term success in the industry.

Resources for Further Learning and Professional Development in the Plumbing Industry

THERE ARE numerous resources available for plumbing professionals looking to expand their knowledge and skills. The following list outlines some valuable resources for further learning and professional development in the plumbing industry:

TRADE ASSOCIATIONS: Joining trade associations such as the Plumbing-Heating-Cooling Contractors Association (PHCC) or the American Society of Plumbing Engineers (ASPE) can provide access to educational resources, networking opportunities, and industry news.

INDUSTRY PUBLICATIONS AND WEBSITES: Stay up-to-date with the latest industry news, trends, and best practices by subscribing to industry publications such as Plumbing & Mechanical Magazine, Contractor Magazine, or Plumbing Engineer. Additionally, websites like Plumber Magazine and PlumbingWeb.com offer valuable online resources.

ONLINE COURSES AND TUTORIALS: There are various online platforms that offer plumbing courses and tutorials, such as Alison, Udemy, and Coursera. These resources can help you learn new skills, explore advanced techniques, and stay current with industry developments.

MANUFACTURER TRAINING: Many manufacturers offer training programs for their products, covering installation, maintenance, and troubleshooting. Contact the manufacturers of the products you use regularly to inquire about available training opportunities.

TRADE SCHOOLS AND COMMUNITY COLLEGES: Trade schools and community colleges often offer plumbing courses and programs for continuing education. These institutions can provide hands-on training, as well as classroom instruction on advanced topics and emerging technologies.

INDUSTRY WORKSHOPS AND SEMINARS: Participate in workshops and seminars hosted by industry organizations, manufacturers, or educational institutions. These events can provide valuable hands-on training, networking opportunities, and insights into the latest industry trends.

APPRENTICESHIPS AND MENTORSHIPS: Consider seeking out apprenticeship or mentorship opportunities with experienced professionals in the industry. Learning from someone with more experience can help you develop advanced skills and gain valuable insights into the trade.

ONLINE FORUMS AND COMMUNITIES: Join online forums and communities related to the plumbing industry, such as PlumbingZone or Terry Love Plumbing & Remodel DIY Forum. These platforms can provide opportunities to connect with other professionals, ask questions, and share your expertise.

SOCIAL MEDIA: Follow industry influencers, trade associations, and manufacturers on social media platforms like LinkedIn, Twitter, and Facebook. This can help you stay informed about industry news, trends, and educational resources.

BOOKS AND MANUALS: Expand your knowledge by reading books and manuals on plumbing techniques, materials, and best practices. Some popular titles include "Modern Plumbing" by E. Keith Blankenbaker, "Plumbing: A Comprehensive Guide" by R. Dodge Woodson, and "Residential Plumbing Basics" by John White.

BY UTILIZING these resources for further learning and professional development, you can continue to grow your skills and knowledge in the plumbing industry. Staying informed and continually developing your expertise will help you stay competitive and enhance your career prospects in this dynamic field.

Need Plumbing Help?
Grab The Companion Books
By Harper Wells

WANT FREE BOOKS?

FREEBOOKDAILY.COM

SOLARTURNSMEON.COM

SKY HIGH ENERGY BILL?

Stop Renting Your Energy, Own It Just Like You Own Your Home

- Solar for **$0 down**
- **Save up to $200/mo** on energy
- **Increase** your home value
- Get **clean renewable energy**
- Get a **30-year warranty**
- **Customized** proposal & best value

Made in United States
Troutdale, OR
04/09/2025